HEROES OF THE WILD WEST

BUFFALO BILL

BY
Simon Boyce

This edition first published by Parragon Books in 1995

Produced by
Magpie Books Ltd, London

Copyright © Parragon Book Service Ltd 1995
Unit 13–17, Avonbridge Trading Estate
Atlantic Road
Avonmouth
Bristol BS11 9QD

Cover pitcure and illustrations courtesy of
Peter Newark's Western Americana

ISBN 0-75250-760-5

A copy of the British Library Cataloguing in Publication
Data is available from the British Library.

Typeset by Hewer Text Composition Services, Edinburgh
Printed in Singapore by Printlink International Co.

HEROES OF THE WILD WEST
Buffalo Bill

Of all the legends that people the mythical American West, few have the stature of Buffalo Bill. The man behind the myth was Colonel William F. Cody. But while Cody was a fairly remarkable man in his own right, the American public demanded an even more heroic character to play the leading role in their dramatized and glorified notion of the push westwards. And so they, together with the dime novelists and hack writers of the period, conjured Buffalo Bill up out of the achievements of Colonel Cody.

Buffalo Bill came to symbolize the American Wild West, the frontier, and the vanquishing of the Redskin by the White man. But as the myth of Buffalo Bill grew, so it gradually submerged William Cody. In his middle life, Cody made his living actually playing Buffalo Bill in a kind of circus, and much of Cody's life was a tussle between his public and private persona. By the end, Cody carried the legend around like a monkey on his back.

The Youngest Indian-Slayer of the Plains

The legend begins in 1857 in Kansas. William F. Cody had been born eleven years earlier. But Buffalo Bill was just coming into being. Despite his tender years, Cody had taken work with the freighting firm of Russell, Majors and Waddell. He was already an accomplished rider and a good shot, and he was capable enough at herding cattle and driving a wagon. The partners in the firm were friends of the family. They had rallied round to find work for young William when his father died, and the boy became the breadwinner of the family.

Russell, Majors and Waddell handled most of the freight heading west through Kansas. They put together wagon trains to ship the supplies and, as the westward-bound traffic grew, so the company expanded. The firm followed a moral code that was something of an anomaly on the frontier in middle of the last century. Employees were forced to sign an oath that they would 'not use profane language, not get drunk, not gamble, not treat animals cruelly and not do anything else that is incompatible with the conduct of a gentleman'. Most of those who signed the oath did so with an 'X'. And it has to be said that in any case a signature didn't count for a whole lot in that environment. Still, the partners were fairly upstanding men. When Cody signed on, Majors said: 'We will take this boy, and we will pay him a man's wages, because he can ride a pony just as well as any man can.' Cody was hired as a 'driving cavayard'; his job was to herd the cattle following the wagons. He was paid $40 a month.

His first assignment was with a wagon train taking supplies to a cavalry force that was trying to subdue a Mormon rebellion. The Mormons were trying to establish an independent community around Salt Lake City, and Washington was determined to stop them. While the train was stopped for the noon halt by a creek near Fort Kearney, it was attacked by a band of Indians. They stampeded the cattle and killed three of Cody's fellow drovers. The train was forced to retreat. The episode that would set Cody on the path to becoming the legendary Buffalo Bill took place as they straggled back to camp along the creek. As young William told it: 'I, being the youngest and smallest of the party, became somewhat tired, and without noticing it, I had fallen behind the others for some little distance. It was about ten o'clock and we were keeping very quiet and hugging close to the bank, when I happened to look up at the moonlit sky and saw the plumed head of an Indian peeping over the bank. Instead of hurrying ahead and alarming the men in a quiet way, I

instantly aimed my gun at his head and
fired. The report rang out sharp and loud
in the night air, and was immediately
followed by an Indian whoop; the next
moment about six feet of dead Indian
came tumbling into the river.'

And so, according to the myth, Buffalo
Bill killed his first Indian at the age of
eleven. As the wagon master, Frank
McCarthy, put it: 'Little Billy has killed
an Indian stone-dead . . . too dead to
skin.' Bill himself claimed later to have
been interviewed by the local paper, the
Leavenworth Times, and, as a result, 'My
name was printed for the first time as the
youngest Indian-slayer of the Plains.'

But, as with other aspects of the Buffalo
Bill myth, the truth seems to have been

buried under the legend. Cody claimed
to have been interviewed in 1857. But
the *Leavenworth Times* wasn't founded
until the following year. There is no
account of the killing in the records of
Russell, Majors and Waddell, nor in the
Annals of Kansas. Still, the event became
a key part of the Buffalo Bill story. As he
put it, with typical eloquence, in later
years: 'That Indian has been hitched to
my name like a tin kettle to a dog's tail.'

It was by no means the only aspect of the
Buffalo Bill legend that had to be taken
with a pinch of salt. The Cody family
also claimed without any supporting
evidence to be descended from the
early kings of Ireland, and it was later
said of Buffalo Bill that 'genuine royal
blood courses in Colonel Cody's veins'.

Beginnings

The Cody family arrived in the United States from Ireland in 1747. They gradually moved westwards, and by the time William was born they had got as far as Iowa. His date of birth, according to the inscription in the family Bible, was 26 February 1846. But his tombstone reckons he appeared in the world a year earlier. His place of birth was the town of Leclair, Iowa.

When William was three, the California gold-rush was gathering speed. His father, Isaac, wasn't much of a farmer, and he had a wife and four children to feed. He caught the gold fever, and in 1853 the family shipped out and headed west. They arrived in Kansas just as the State was becoming a battleground in the fight between the Abolitionists and the pro-slavery Southerners.

Isaac built a log cabin on the family claim by a major trail heading west to Utah and the California gold-fields. He promptly got involved in the local politics, which were heating up with the slavery issue. The local paper gave some idea of the kind of passions involved: 'I tell you,' growled one editorial, 'mark every scoundrel

among you that is the least tainted
with free-soilism, or Abolitionism,
and exterminate him.' Well, Isaac
Cody was more than tainted by Abolitionism, and the local community
was strongly pro-slavery. He had a
taste, and a gift, for rhetoric. At one
meeting, after arguing against slavery
before a hostile crowd, he was stabbed
in the back by a drunken political
opponent.

He died sometime later, leaving his son
William to fend for the family. 'We had
now been reduced to utter destitution,'
Cody junior wrote later. 'Our only fare
was what rabbits and birds I could trap
and catch with the help of our faithful
old dog Turk, and the sod corn we
grated into flour.'

Buffalo Bill Cody in his early frontier days.

The Wagon Boss, Charles M. Russell.

Riding with the Russell, Majors and Waddell wagon trains enabled Bill to provide for the family for a while. But his mother worried about his education. In the winter of 1857–8 she insisted he attend the local school. He was already big for his age, and not a committed student. 'The master of the frontier school wore out several armfuls of hazel switches in a vain effort to interest me in the three Rs', he said.

Riding with the Pony Express

The death of his father, and moving in a man's world, forced young Bill to grow up quickly. He was enthralled by life on the trail, and by the military who at that time were swarming around the frontier. He would hang around Fort Laramie, effectively the capital of 'Indian' country, an outpost surrounded by thousands of Sioux, Cheyenne and Arapaho Indians.

Despite the efforts of the local school-
master, William Cody got his real
schooling at the hands of the tough
frontiersmen who hung out at Fort
Laramie. Among them was Kit
Carson, one of the most famous scouts
and Indian-hunters in the West. Despite
the harsh life he led, Carson was a small
and fastidious man, quiet and dapper. He
fascinated Cody, so much so that the
latter named his only son after him.
Carson and his fellow frontiersmen
taught young William how to find his
way in the wilderness without maps,
how to survive with just a knife and a
gun, and how to get along with the
Indians. He also learned how to drink.
His sister relates how the young man
once came home with a skinful, shout-
ing that he would become president of

the United States. The next morning, his head was swollen with a hangover rather than aspirations to high office, and, according to his sister, 'Will never touched hard cider again.' That may be true, but he certainly didn't stop drinking. For years he needed ten tumblers of whisky a day to keep his kidneys functioning properly, he said. In later life, he recalled one occasion when he had returned home stone-cold sober to find the door of his house locked. He'd called out in a steady voice to his wife to let him in. But she refused to believe it was him; she was so used to his coming home the worse for drink. So he went off to the local sutler's, got roaring drunk, and went home to try again. 'Then I fell up against the door like a bale of hay and shouted for my wife.

"Oh, is that you, Willy? I'm so glad you're home," my wife said, and she let me in.'

When he wasn't with the scouts and Indian-hunters, young Cody spent his time playing with local Sioux children, and began to pick up their language. He would also hang out on the nearby Kickapoo reservation, playing with the Indian kids there. In fact, most of the childhood playmates of the world's most famous Indian-killer were Indians.

At thirteen, life taught William Cody a lesson. He set off on a trapping and hunting trip with his close friend Dave Harrington. They set up camp about 200 miles west of the Cody home-stead, and had a fair success with the game. But they then caught something else – gold fever. They traipsed through the mountains digging and panning for a time, but without success. Disheartened, Cody returned home, but Harrington remained at the camp, where he then caught pneumonia and died. Cody seems to have decided that this event was significant. If you could survive all the perils of the frontier, and still succumb to a common cold, you might as well live dangerously.

Among the more dangerous jobs then going in the Wild West was riding the Pony Express, and young Will duly signed up. The Express was a subsidiary of the Russell, Majors and Waddell operation. These were days before the railways had made it out West, before even the telegraph poles loped across the prairies. The Pony Express provided a kind of madcap, express postal service. Teams of riders on the fastest ponies relayed mail from St Joseph, Missouri, to Sacramento, California, a distance of around 2,000 miles. The riders were expected to cover something like 250 miles a day, averaging up to 15 miles an hour. But it wasn't just the gruelling ride that made the job of Pony Express rider hard and dangerous work. They were also constantly at risk of ambush and attack by Indians. In fact, although Cody started out with a relatively short route of 45 miles, so many riders were picked off that his section was lengthened to 76 miles.

The attacks on riders were viewed as a threat to business by the Pony Express managers, and they decided to organize a punitive expedition. Young Cody signed up, as did his sidekick, Wild Bill Hickok. They set off up the Powder River, until they spied out an Indian encampment. They had no idea whether these people were in any way connected with the attacks on Russell, Majors and Waddell riders and wagon trains. But, nonetheless, the White men waited until nightfall and then rode into the camp, shooting at anything that moved, including women and children. It's not known how many of the Indians were killed, but the horsemen did make off with a hundred ponies that ostensibly belonged to their bosses. Cody described the sortie as a 'grand spree', and celebrated it with four days of drinking that only wound up when the booze ran out.

Pony Express poster of 1861.

Pony Express rider pursued by Indians, by H.W. Hansen.

To put Cody's Indian hunting experiences into some kind of context, it's worth mentioning the findings of a President's Commission in 1869. The commission found that 'The history of the border White man's connection with the Indians is a sickening record of murder, outrage, robbery and wrongs committed by the former, as a rule, and occasional savage outbreaks and unspeakably barbarous deeds of retaliation by the latter, as the exception.' But William was indoctrinated with the border ideology. The Indian was less than a human being, who could be killed like a pest, and should be slaughtered if he got in the way of the White man's progress.

Mrs Buffalo Bill

Cody's lifestyle was beginning to take its toll on his character. At eighteen, he wrote, 'I was becoming a very hard case . . . leading a dissolute and reckless life with gamblers, drunkards and bad characters generally.' He wasn't likely to encounter anybody more upstanding when he joined up to fight for the Yankees in the American Civil War. According to the purple prose of Buffalo Bill's biographers, he enjoyed a distinguished military career. In actual fact, his major achievement was to make it from recruit to full private – the next lowest rank.

He enlisted while he was drunk, during a bout of revelry with soldiers from the Kansas volunteers. It wasn't until the next day that he realized what he had done: 'Under the influence of bad whisky, I awoke to find myself a soldier in the 7th Kansas. I did not remember how or when I had enlisted, but I saw I was in for it, and that it would not do for me to endeavour to back out.'

Cody's biographers maintain that he served as a spy – for which he could have been shot – and gathered intelligence which proved vital to the Union cause, and that he served valiantly in the Battle of Pilot's Knob, among other feats. In fact, there was no such battle in the Civil War. And his contributions to espionage were ignored by the Official Record of the War of the Rebellion. Indeed, the 7th Kansas saw only eight minor engagements and lost only five casualties during the entire war.

However, he did manage one important encounter. He met his wife, Louisa Frederici, while his unit was waiting at the rear, in St Louis. Again, according to those who fashioned the Buffalo Bill myth, their first meeting was the stuff of romantic novels. They reputedly met when Cody rescued her from the un-wanted attentions of a bunch of drunken soldiers: 'With one blow of his clenched hand he dashed the bulky miscreant to the earth, with his other arm he encircled the waist of the lovely girl, and lifting her to his saddle-bow, gave the word "on" to his noble horse . . .'

Louisa's account is a little different. She remembers that her cousin asked if he could introduce her to a young soldier, to which she agreed. Later, she was sitting drowsing in her parlour, in front of the fire, when someone pulled the chair out from under her. She leapt up to see a strange young man grinning at her. She slapped him across the cheek and flounced from the room. But Cody, for it was he, later apologized, and Louisa found herself attracted to 'about the most handsome man I had ever seen'. Reportedly, his claim to have killed an

Indian at the age of eleven also made a big impression.

Despite this physical attraction, Louisa and Cody were about as different as a couple can be. All she wanted was quiet domesticity, a comfortable home, financial security, an orderly life – all things which were anathema to Cody. Quiet domesticity drove him insane. He thirsted for adventure, was profligate with what money he had and was an incurable exhibitionist. Nonetheless, the two were married, despite the misgivings of the bride's father, on 6 March 1866, and Cody whisked his new wife off to Kansas on a paddle-steamer.

The Codys set up shop at the Golden Rule Hotel in Leavenworth, where

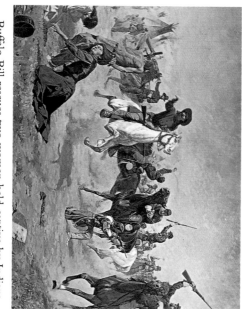

Buffalo Bill rescues two women held captive by Indians.

Hunting buffalo with Grand Duke Alexis of Russia.

Bill's golden rule seemed to be to hold a party every night with free drinks for his mates. He offered the hotel's hospitality to his sisters, then more distant family, and then to his drinking partners, and seemed to think that charging for a room was a breach of manners. As his sister Helen commented, 'Socially he was an irreproachable landlord, but financially his shortcomings were deplorable.'

Colonel Cody Earns the Name 'Buffalo Bill'

In the end, it became apparent that Cody wasn't cut out to be a hotelier. After six months he sold up, kissed his wife goodbye and went off to work on the railroad, then unrolling across the country. He soon met up again with Wild Bill Hickok, and the two of them looked for work scouting with the army. At this time, the combative Plains Indians – the Cheyenne, Arapaho,

Comanche and Sioux – were bitterly resisting the encroachment of the White man. The army needed good scouts, and such men were scarce. Even undesirables like Cody, Carson and Hickok were sought after. In fact, the chief of the frontier command, Major-General Philip H. Sheridan, singled Cody out for his 'endurance and courage'.

In 1867, Louisa gave birth to the Codys' first daughter, Arta. But Bill was just then taking time out from scouting to sign up for a get-rich-quick scheme. He and a partner had surveyed an area of land near Fort Hays, and staked it out into town lots. They called the incipient community 'Rome'. He wrote to Louisa to come and join him, saying he would soon be worth $250,000.

Unfortunately for the property specula-
tors, the land-agent for the Kansas
Pacific Railroad had established Hays
City one mile away. The railroad repair
shops meant plenty of jobs, and the
citizens of Rome began to decamp
for Hays City. Cody returned from a
hunt one day to see his town disappear-
ing before his eyes: 'The town was
being literally torn down and carted
away. The balloon-frame buildings
were coming apart section by section.
I could see at least a hundred teams and
wagons carting lumber, furniture and
everything that made up the town over
the prairies to the eastward.' Louisa
promptly returned to her mother in
St Louis, and Cody went off to become Buffalo Bill by exterminating
buffalo.

The extension of the railroad westward meant an army of graders, track-layers and section-hands marching across the prairies. These men had to be fed as cheaply as possible, and the herds of buffalo yielded a plentiful supply of meat, providing they could be caught.

The Kansas City firm of Goddard Bros. hired Cody to hunt the animals. He was paid $500 a month, which was good money in those days. For that, he had to kill at least 12 buffalo a day. Only the beast's hump and the hind-quarters were considered edible. The rest was left to rot where it lay. During the decade following the Civil War, Cody and his colleagues killed millions of buffalo, devastating the herds. Since the Indians derived much of their livelihood from the buffalo, this meant the wrecking of their way of life. General Sheridan, Bill's commander, claimed that the White buffalo hunters did more to 'settle the Indian question' than the army did in thirty years.

Actually, to say that the buffalo were hunted is to exaggerate the role of their killers. Buffalo are stupid and slow. And Bill was an excellent shot with his 50-calibre Springfield rifle. Knocking off twelve of the animals a day was hardly taxing. In fact, during a shooting contest with another 'hunter', Bill picked off 69 buffalo in one afternoon. He later named his hunting rifle 'Lucrezia Borgia', after the evil daughter of the scheming Italian family.

Having done his bit to wreck the ecosystem of the Plains, Buffalo Bill went back to scouting for his old boss, Sheridan. He was highly valued by the general for his horsemanship and his endurance. He once rode 350 miles in three days on various scouting duties. Bill was also a capable scout, and Sheridan appointed him Chief of Scouts for the 5th Cavalry.

The legend of Buffalo Bill was beginning to grow. But while those who wrote up his life made out that he single-handedly mowed down Redskins and generally lived the life of a Wild West hero, his actual exploits were less mythic. On one occasion, he and Hickok took time out from taming the West to hijack a pack-train laden with beer for the soldiers at

Fort Evans. Bill and Hickok decided that they and the 5th Cavalry were more deserving than their fellows, and decided to 'requisition' the beer, which they then sold by the pint to the 5th. 'The result', said Bill, 'was one of the biggest beer jollifications it has ever been my misfortune to attend.'

Around this time, Buffalo Bill grew his hair to his shoulders, and also grew a goatee and a handlebar moustache. All this hirsuteness was a mark of honour among men like Bill and General Custer – it was a hairy defiance of the Indian's keenness to scalp them.

Buffalo Bill the Celebrity

The legend of Buffalo Bill owes at least as much to the efforts of hacks and dime-novel writers as it does to the exploits of the man himself. Scribes like Ned Buntline saw it as their job to provide the folks back east with suitably larger-than-life tales of hardy men taming the Wild West. Buffalo Bill was just the extravagant figure they needed, as well as being in real life at least something like the kind of hero they were looking for. As a

result, descriptions of his life and deeds –
appropriately glorified – were scrawled
by the dozen. Works such as *Buffalo Bill
and His Daring Adventures in the Romantic
Wild West*, by Nebraska Ned, sold well.
Colonel Prentiss Ingraham churned out
203 Buffalo Bill novels.

Unfortunately, the accounts of Bill's
feats provided by these chroniclers
rarely agreed. For instance, Buffalo Bill
was variously reported as having killed
Chief Tall Bull by shooting him at close
quarters, by shooting him 'from fully
400 yards', and by stabbing him with a
knife. Bill himself claims that, after
having killed the chief, he was enter-
tained to tea by the man's wife and
family. He asserted that Mrs Tall Bull
'esteemed it quite an honour that her

One of the many 'dime' novels that spread
the legend of Buffalo Bill.

Buffalo Bill Cody at the height of his fame.

husband, a great warrior himself, should have met his death at my hands'. In fact, Chief Tall Bull was killed Major Frank North. North later accepted a co-starring role in Buffalo Bill's Wild West Show, and at each performance had to stand by while Bill re-enacted *his* brave killing of Chief Tall Bull.

After scouting for a while, Bill settled down for some time with his wife and daughter. Such was his fame that he was selected as Justice of the Peace for the small town of McPherson, Kansas. His notion of justice was a little unorthodox. A horse-thief, for example, was fined $20 for his misdemeanour. 'I pocketed the $20, of course,' admitted Bill. 'Some people might think it was not a square way of doing business, but

I didn't know any better just then.' It also fell to him to perform weddings, an obligation for which he prepared by 'imbibing rather freely of stimulants'. He would end the ceremony by proclaiming: 'I now pronounce you to be man and wife, and whomsoever God and Buffalo Bill have joined together, let no man put asunder.'

At this time, it was fashionable for easterners to head west to rub shoulders with Wild West characters, sleep under the stars, execute buffalo, and generally pretend they were cowboys for a couple of days. Bill managed to get work scouting for one of these 'dude' parties, 'a nobby and high-toned outfit' as he described it. Although the Yankees wanted to get an idea of life on the frontier, that didn't mean they had to forgo every comfort. One of their dinners, eaten out on the range, consisted of:

Buffalo tail soup
Broiled cisco; fried dace
Salmi of prairie dog; stewed rabbit;
filet of buffalo aux champignons
Sweet potatoes, mashed potatoes,
green peas
Tapioca pudding
Champagne frappé, champaign [*sic*]
au naturel, claret
Whisky, brandy and ale
Coffee

Buffalo Bill realized that wet-nursing these easterners was more lucrative and less hazardous than scouting for the cavalry. One of the young and wealthy men

in his party also decided that Bill would be
good value back in New York. After he
returned east, he sent Bill a railroad pass,
$500 in cash and a spray of invitations to
the best homes on the eastern seaboard.
So, in 1872, Bill left the prairies to join the
urban fancy set. He made his first appearance in society in Chicago, decked out in
a dinner-suit, a stetson, and a fur coat
given to him by Grand Duke Alexis of
Russia, who had been on one of the
hunting trips that Bill led. 'When I was
escorted in, I was told to give the coloured
boy my hat and coat. To this I violently
objected. I prized the coat beyond all my
earthly possessions, and intended to take
no chances with it.' He managed to
shuffle and stomp his way through one
dance, but that was enough. 'As soon as it
was over, I hurriedly escorted my fair

Buffalo Bill scalps Chief Yellowhand.

A group of cowboys from the Wild West Show.

partner to her seat, then I quickly made
my way to the bar room. The man behind
the bar appreciated my plight. He stowed
me away behind the icebox and in that
corner I remained for the rest of the
evening.'

He then moved on to New York, where
he made a splash as an exotic specimen
from the wilds of the West. He was wined
and dined and interviewed incessantly.
Stories of his exploits filled the society
pages and columns. When he went to
the theatre, a spotlight was shone on his
box, and he was given a standing ovation.
One of the shows he attended was 'Buffalo
Bill, the King of the Border Men', more or
less a pantomime dramatization of his own
deeds of derring-do. The manager of the
theatre stepped into his box and offered

him $500 a week to play the lead, por-
traying himself. But Bill said, 'You might
as well try to make an actor out of a
government mule.'

So intense was the interest in Buffalo Bill
that he could be said to be America's first
real celebrity, in the twentieth-century
sense of the word. He was adulated,
pointed at and gossiped about. Soon
his public persona took on an existence
independent of the man himself. Even
he didn't know where William Cody
stopped and Buffalo Bill began.

After a time, he began to tire of the
constant attention, of the soirées and
balls and dinners, of being paraded in
front of one society set after another.
On the way to one such gathering, he

'became badly demoralized and confused'. In other words, he stopped off at a number of hostelries *en route* to the function to fortify himself. He turned up late and somewhat the worse for wear. But he excused himself by saying he had 'gone out on a scout and got lost'.

He was summoned away from the social whirl of New York City by a telegram. He was urgently required to take up the post of Chief Scout to the 3rd Cavalry. The Sioux had been getting uppity, and the 3rd was going on a punitive mission. It was due to his exploits during this time that he was later awarded the Congressional Medal of Honor. When the Sioux had calmed down a bit he was elected to the Nebraska legislature, although he never took up his seat.

From Frontiersman to Showman

The blurring line between William Cody and Buffalo Bill was further confused when his inventive biographer Ned Buntline invited him back to Chicago to play himself in a show. In 1872, Bill packed up his family and set off for the 'windy city'. Things got off to a bad start. Bill failed to bring the twenty authentic Indians he'd agreed to provide for the show, and Buntline had failed to

write a single line of the script, even
though the first night was less than a
week away. Still, Ned's failure was easily
remedied. He holed himself up in a
hotel room, and afterwards boasted that
he wrote the show, 'Scout of the Plains',
in four hours. He asked Bill how long it
would take him to learn his lines. 'About
seven years,' Bill replied. 'With good
luck.' In fact, he had four days.

Not surprisingly, the first performance
was a little ragged. But Buffalo Bill simply
had to appear on the stage to keep the
audience happy. The three acts were
largely variations on a single theme –
Bill and his fellow scouts trouncing the
Indians. But the paying public was happy.
The take that night was $2,800. The
critics were less impressed. The *Chicago*

Times wrote, 'such a combination of incongruous drama, execrable acting, renowned performers, intolerable stench, scalping, blood and thunder is not likely to be vouchsafed to a city a second time – even Chicago.'

Nonetheless, the public loved it, and the show went on to successful runs in St Louis, Cincinnati, Albany and Boston. In St Louis, the cast was temporarily arrested on a riot charge. In Cincinnati, one of the cast died after a punch-up on stage. Despite these setbacks, the show moved on to New York City. There, the reception was mixed. The *New York Herald* said: 'The Hon. William F. Cody, otherwise "Buffalo Bill", occasionally called by the refined people of the eastern cities

Poster for the Wild West Show.

Portrait of Wild Bill Hickok by H.H. Cross.

"Bison William", is a good-looking fellow, tall and straight as an arrow, but ridiculous as an actor.'

Despite his limitations as an actor, Buffalo Bill was a commercial success. But Ned Buntline was a liability. Fortunately, at this time along came Major John Burke, a.k.a. Arizona John. He'd never actually been to Arizona, and he had no obvious claim to the title 'Major'. But he was good news for Buffalo Bill. 'I have met a god,' said Burke on first meeting Bill. He'd worked as a newspaperman and as the manager of an acrobatic troupe. He was an ideal candidate to be Buffalo Bill's agent and PR representative, as Bill made the change from frontiersman to showman.

His slavering descriptions of Bill were extraordinarily over the top. After that first meeting, he described the one-time Indian-killer in glistening terms. 'Physically superb, trained to the limit, in the zenith of his manhood, features cast in nature's most perfect mold, on a prancing charger that was foaming and chafing at the bit, and in his most picturesque beaded buckskin garb, he was indeed a picture. When he dismounted I was introduced to the finest specimen of God's handiwork I had ever seen, and felt that for once there was that nearest approach to an ideal human, a visual interpretation given to the assertion that man was indeed a replica of his Maker.' Burke's oratorical skills combined the styles of a music-hall barker and romance novelist. He was an ideal

choice as the mouthpiece of the bloom-
ing Buffalo Bill myth.

'Scout of the Plains' was rewritten. The
Ned Buntline character was dropped
and Wild Bill Hickok was persuaded
to come east and play himself. He'd
been working as Marshal of Abilene
and Hays City, Kansas. But his sight
was going, and he was sacked after
mistakenly gunning down one of his
own deputies. If Buffalo Bill was an
unlikely Thespian, Hickok was posi-
tively preposterous. He regarded 'play
acting' as unmanly, and refused to follow
the script or the plot. He also had to say
things like 'Fear not, fair maid! By
Heavens, you are safe with Wild Bill,
who is ever ready to risk his life and die,
if need be, in defence of weak and

defenceless womanhood!' He was followed around the stage by a spotlight, which he hated. He took to hiding behind the scenery to say his lines, and eventually threw his pistol at the light, scoring a direct hit. During another performance, Wild Bill, Buffalo Bill and others were sitting around a camp-fire, drinking from a whisky bottle. As is standard, the whisky had been replaced by cold tea. But Wild Bill decided the pretence had gone on long enough. He spat the liquid out and shouted, 'You must think I'm the biggest fool east of the Rockies that I can't tell whisky from cold tea.' Eventually Hickok abandoned the stage.

The Duel with Chief Yellow Hand

In 1876, Buffalo Bill's acting career was also interrupted. His son, Kit, died of scarlet fever. The boy, who was only six, was the apple of Bill's eye. Grief-stricken, Bill gave up the frivolous world of the theatre and went back West. Trouble was brewing again on the Plains. In the Dakotas, Wyoming and Montana, the Sioux and the Cheyenne were again on the warpath, after

the government had reneged on another treaty. Washington had promised
that the Black Hills of South Dakota
would always be reserved for the Indians, who held the hills to be sacred.
But rumours of gold there had led to a
stampede of prospectors. Early in the
year, Chiefs Sitting Bull and Crazy
Horse and other leaders gathered thousands of warriors for a war of resistance.
This time they were using a new tactic,
coordinating the rival tribes into one
force, under Sitting Bull. They
achieved considerable success. One of
the engagements of these wars was the
Battle of Little Bighorn, where General
Custer's force was wiped out.

Buffalo Bill arrived to take up his post as
scout with the 5th Cavalry wearing the

Buffalo Bill and the 'Deadwood' coach
which featured in his show.

Postcard printed during Buffalo Bill's visit
to Britain in 1903.

costume from his theatrical troupe – a black velvet and gold uniform, decorated with silver lace, and topped off with a plumed sombrero.

It was during these Indian wars that another episode in the Buffalo Bill legend occurred. At one point, the 5th Cavalry found itself confronting a Cheyenne war party, made up of 800 warriors. For some reason, both sides decided that the outcome of their encounter should be determined by a duel. Buffalo Bill was the man chosen to represent the US troops. His opponent was a young Cheyenne chief called Yellow Hand. The latter rode out from the body of Indians and called out a challenge: 'I know you, Pahaska. If you want to fight, come out and fight with me.' 'Pahaska' means 'long yellow hair' in the language of the Cheyennes, a reference to Bill's flowing locks.

Yellow Hand was decked out in a manner guaranteed to offend the White man. He was wearing an American flag as a loincloth, and from his belt dangled the bloody scalp of a blonde woman. Bill accepted his challenge, and the two galloped towards one another. Bill fired, and killed Yellow Hand's horse. The young warrior leapt clear, and then Bill's horse tripped. The two men now faced each other at a distance of about 20 yards. Both fired, and Buffalo Bill proved the better shot. Yellow Hand missed, but Bill hit the Indian in the chest. He leapt on Yellow Hand and finished him off with a knife. He then mutilated him. 'Jerking off his war bonnet I scientifically scalped him in about five seconds.' He turned to his comrades, brandishing the grisly trophy, and shouted, 'The first scalp for Custer.'

According to some accounts of the duel, Yellow Hand was armed only with a tomahawk, which would rather diminish Buffalo Bill's heroism. But the version that later made it into Buffalo Bill's Wild West Show had Yellow Hand fully armed.

Bill later decided to send the scalp of Yellow Hand to his wife (now living in Rochester, New York) perhaps as a token of his love, perhaps as physical evidence of his accomplishments. She later recalled how, when she prised the box open, 'A terrific odour reached my nostrils . . . I reeled slightly – then reached for the contents. Then I fainted. For I had brought from that box the raw, red scalp of an Indian.'

Bill later followed the scalp back east, to appear in a new dramatic celebration of his latest feat, 'The Red Right Hand, or Buffalo Bill's First Scalp for Custer'. He went on to perform in a number of highly successful productions. According to Major John Burke, Bill made around $135,000 over a seven-year period. He bought himself a huge ranch in Nebraska. But he never managed to save much of his money. He described himself as the beneficiary of 'immense success and comparative wealth'. Despite the fact that these

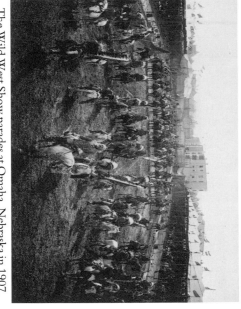

The Wild West Show parades at Omaha, Nebraska in 1907.

Poster of 1910 showing the history of the Wild West Show.

shows were little more than a glorifica-
tion of his own deeds, Bill began to tire
of the self-aggrandizement and charla-
tanry. 'Oh, Nellie,' he said to his sister.
'Don't say anything about it. If heaven
will forgive me for this foolishness, I
promise to quit it for ever as soon as
this season is finished.'

In fact, he did the opposite. He went on
to participate in an even more exagger-
ated depiction of the Wild West and the
role he played in taming it. This new
fandango was Buffalo Bill's Wild West
Show.

Buffalo Bill's Wild West Show

In 1882, Buffalo Bill recruited a part-time dentist and full-time sharpshooter named Doc Carver to his show. He was a brilliant marksman, who could hit a nickel thrown in the air. His other great talent was self-promotion. He claimed the Indians called him 'the Evil Spirit of the Plains' because of his deeds. His egotism guaranteed that his relationship with Bill would be one of jealous rivalry. But Carver had $80,000 to invest in the show, so Bill managed to keep quiet as Carver sounded off and, early in May 1883, 'The Wild West, Rocky Mountain and Prairie Expedition' set out for Omaha, Nebraska, for its first engagement. John Burke had outdone himself with the playbills: 'The Grassy Sward our Carpet, Heaven's Azure Canopy our Canvas, No Tinsel, No Gilding, No Humbug, No Sideshows or Freaks.'

Despite the success of the show, Bill was going through a bad patch. As a colleague in the show described him, 'He had been sleeping on the floor of a tent in some hay, his fur coat was missing, his hair was all matted and he was drunk . . . Colonel Cody was drunk every day for our first five weeks out.'

The show was also having problems with Carver. He was incredibly short-tempered, and would get into a rage if his shooting was off. In fact, the show was falling apart, what with Buffalo Bill's drinking and his disagreements with Carver. Then tragedy struck the Cody family again. His daughter Orra, who had been born in 1872, followed Kit Cody to the grave. Bill hit a new low and he and Carver decided to part company.

But Bill was fortunate enough to have met the manager of a rival troupe, Nate Salsbury, who shared his dream of a full-blown Wild West extravaganza. He signed a partnership agreement with Salsbury and, together with Burke, the two men went about establishing Buffalo Bill's Wild West Show. Again,

Burke brought his copywriting prowess to bear. The show was 'the Romantic West brought East in Reality . . . Each Scene Instructive . . . A Year's Visit West in Three Hours'.

The Wild West Show had its first engagement in St Louis. Doc Carver had a rival outfit that had just finished its run there. He took out adverts in the local papers, warning the populace against Buffalo Bill: 'He who loves Wine and Women, and Indulges to Excess, is not a fit Representative of Mankind to appear before the Public as an Instructor of Refined Women and Children.'

Bill was certainly indulging in wine. When the show moved on to Pittsburg, he had to take to his bed because 'my liver flopped'. The show travelled to New York, where the newspapers were almost unanimously enthusiastic, although they did wonder about the number of times the Indians in the performance were slaughtered and then rose from the dead to be re-slaughtered. But, despite the critical success, the Wild West Show was losing money badly. The summer of 1884 was wet and cold, which spelled disaster for a show staged outdoors, and the vendetta with Carver was sapping the show morally and financially. However, rescue was at hand, for the show's fortunes were about to be dramatically turned around by the appearance on the scene of two new performers.

Little Annie Oakley
and Chief Sitting Bull

It was Burke who found Little Annie
Oakley. She was half of a sharpshooting
team, the other half being her husband.
She was five feet tall and weighed less
than a hundred pounds. But in her
stetson and shooting blouse covered
with medals for marksmanship, she
soon became the star of the Wild West
Show. Her skill with a gun was remarkable. She could hit a playing card held

edge-on by her husband at 30 yards. Sighting in a mirror, she could fire over her shoulder and smash a glass ball that her husband whirled around his head on a piece of string. Once, using three 16-gauge shotguns, she broke 4,772 out of 5,000 glass balls tossed in the air over a period of nine hours.

The other major attraction of the 1885–6 season was Chief Sitting Bull. He was a daring choice by the show's managers. Most White people knew him only as 'the killer of Custer'. But he was a huge draw, sitting calmly, squat and fierce, with a face like a tomahawk, dressed in a brocade waistcoat, a huge crucifix dangling round his neck. He detested being on display. But he and his family back on the Standing Rock Reservation needed money. He also liked two things about life in the eastern cities – oyster stew and boiled sweets. Most of the money he earned he either sent back west, or gave to the destitute children he saw in the cities. He could not understand why all the wealth he saw in the cities wasn't divided up among the poor.

Before Sitting Bull returned to the West he helped turn the Wild West Show into a huge success. By now, Nate Salsbury had perfected the logistics of the operation. He had obtained a special train with 26 cars, painted white, inscribed with 'Buffalo Bill's Wild West Show' in gold lettering. They carried all 240 performers and backstage staff, the livestock, a portable grandstand, a huge backcloth painted with the Wyoming mountains, and the lighting system.

The show steamed into New York, where it sold out. Among those who saw it there were Civil War hero General Sherman, General Custer's widow, and Mark Twain. Twain was glowing in his praise and suggested that Buffalo Bill take his spectacular abroad. In 1887, the outfit travelled to England.

Buffalo Bill wows
Queen Victoria

The British embraced Buffalo Bill and his show. That may partly have been because of John Burke's advertising campaign. He pasted up so many bills all over London that one journalist commented:

'I may walk it, or bus it, or hansom
    cab it; still
I am faced by the features of
    Buffalo Bill;

Every hoarding is plastered from
    East End to West
With his hat, coat and counte-
    nance, lovelocks and vest.'

The show's 97 Indians fascinated the
Londoners. William Gladstone, who'd
been Prime Minister until a few months
before, visited the troupe, and, after
smoking a cigar with Buffalo Bill, sought
out Chief Red Shirt. According to an
eavesdropping journalist, Gladstone asked
the Indian what he thought of the English
weather, to which Red Shirt replied that
he couldn't complain so far.

A command performance was arranged
for the Prince of Wales. The Prince was
so impressed that he recommended the
show to his mother, Queen Victoria.

She in turn demanded a command performance, at which would be present an array of European monarchs. On 12 May 1887, she led a convoy of royalty from Windsor Castle to the show site. When the show began, Bill rode into the arena bearing a huge Stars and Stripes, to which Queen Victoria bowed. John Burke announced later: 'For the first time since the Declaration of Independence, a Sovereign of Great Britain saluted the Star-Spangled Banner – and that banner was carried by Buffalo Bill.' After the show, the company was presented to the Queen, who told Annie Oakley, 'You are a very, very clever little girl.'

The sovereign was so overwhelmed by the Wild West Show that she requested an unprecedented second command performance, to be held at Windsor Castle. The show featured a stage-coach, which was attacked by a band of Indians. On this occasion, riding shot-gun next to Buffalo Bill, was the Prince of Wales, while inside the coach were the Kings of Denmark, Saxony, Greece and Austria. Bill later wrote to his wife, 'I've just held four Kings! And I was the joker! It wasn't a card game either . . . We sure did rock around that arena, with the Indians yelling and shooting behind us fit to kill . . . I wouldn't want to say it out loud – but I'm pretty sure that before the ride was over, most of the Kings were under the seat.'

After wowing the royalty, Bill was vir-tually crowned himself. Such was his relationship with Queen Victoria that they were even rumoured to be having an affair. He became a social sensation in London. It was said that Oscar Wilde was pouting with envy at the amount of attention Bill was getting. *The Times* wrote that 'Colonel Cody has done his part to bring America and England together', and claimed for some reason that 'civilization itself consents to march in the train of Buffalo Bill'.

In the summer of 1889, the Wild West Show set off on a tour of the Continent. The show was a roaring success in Paris, where among those who attended were the Sultan of Turkey, the Shah of Persia, and the King of Senegal. The latter reportedly tried to buy Little Annie Oakley from Buffalo Bill for 100,000

francs to help him control a plague of
tigers in his homeland.

The Germans were fascinated by Buffalo
Bill's Wild West. But the company was
mystified by the interest shown in the
show by the German military. Annie
Oakley wrote in her diary: 'We never
moved without at least 40 officers of the
Prussian Guard standing all about with
notebooks, taking down every detail of
the performance . . . But most of all
they took interest in our kitchen. The
travelling ranges were inspected and
enumerated in those endless notebooks. The chefs were interviewed.
The methods of storing food, of prepar-
ing it, of having necessities ready for use
at a minute's notice, all these things were
jotted down . . . We had no idea, of

course, that the world was to listen, mouths open, twenty-five years later to the stories of the marvellous travelling kitchens of the Teuton army, serving meals piping hot on the road to Belgium.'

Buffalo Bill's Last Years

In 1892, Buffalo Bill and his Wild West Show returned to the United States. By now, Bill was weary and jaded by life on the road, despite the adulation and celebrity status that went with it. But he was chained to the show by his financial commitments. He spent the money as fast as it came in – which was fast. The show made a million dollars during its stint in New York that year. But Bill frittered his fortune away on poor investments and self-indulgence. He spent his money building the town of Cody, Wyoming, he bought ranches and other landholdings, he bought a mine, and he gave, loaned and drank away much of the rest. It was estimated that his total investments amounted to $1,000,000. But none of them ever made a consistent profit.

Things were beginning to go wrong with the show as well. On Christmas Eve, 1902, Nate Salsbury died. He had been the managerial and financial genius behind the show, and without him it would never be the same operation. The Buffalo Bill Wild West version of events was also losing out to the movies, which were then just appearing, and which could portray the mythical

West much more vividly, if no more authentically.

In the end, plagued by debt and ill health, Bill was forced to auction off the show's assets. His kidneys were failing, his heart was giving out, and he suffered from rheumatism and prostate problems. Against his wishes, Buffalo Bill was finally confined to bed at his sister's house in Denver.

Just before the end, Bill asked his doctor how much longer he had. 'About thirty-six hours, sir,' the man replied. On hearing that, Bill hoisted himself up on his pillows and yelled for his brother-in-law. 'The doc says I've got thirty-six hours,' he said. 'Let's forget about it and play some cards.'

Four days later, on 10 January 1917, Buffalo Bill died. Or rather, William Cody died. Because Buffalo Bill lives on, a hero of the Wild West, a legend of the frontier and a key player in America's notion of itself.